KTG know the game

Golf

Produced in collaboration with
The Professional Golfers' Association

Rules of Golf by Courtesy of the
Royal and Ancient Golf Club, St. Andrews

Published by A & C Black (Publishers) Ltd
35 Bedford Row, London WC1R 4JH

GW00360254

Contents

Foreword	2
The Game	4
Etiquette	4
The Club and the Ball	5
Stance	8
The Grip	10
Making the Stroke	12
Rules of the Game	14
Putting	32
Keeping the Score	33
Etiquette	35
Definitions	36

Paul Way

Foreword

The origins of the game of golf have been the subject of much research for many years and still arouse controversy.

It is considered that the game began in Scotland, although several landscapes painted by Dutch and Flemish artists suggest that golf was played in Holland before it was known in Scotland.

The first mention of the game in official records was during the Scottish Parliaments of 1457–1491 when golf was prohibited due to its popularity interfering with the practice of archery, to the consequent detriment of the national defence in the wars against England; by the reign of James II golf had become a national pastime in Scotland.

The Honourable Company of Edinburgh Golfers situated at Muirfield formed the first set of Rules of the game, and these were adopted by the Society of St. Andrews Golfers which was formed in 1754.

In 1834 King William IV approved the change of name of the Society to the Royal and Ancient Golf Club of St. Andrews, which is responsible for the government of the game, the interpretation of the Rules and the control of the Open Championship.

The following organisations are responsible for the control of amateur golf in their respective areas: The English Golf Union (founded 1924), The Golfing Union of Ireland (founded 1891), The Scottish Golf Union (founded 1920) and the Welsh Golfing Union (founded 1895).

With the spread of the game overseas many organisations have been formed, the most significant being the United States Golf Association founded in 1894, which is responsible for governing all aspects of the game in America and has close contact with the Royal and Ancient Golf Club to maintain uniformity in the administration of the game.

In 1927 Mr. Samuel Ryder presented the Ryder Cup for competition between the professionals from America and Britain, and the contest takes place in alternate years, each country being visited in turn. Since 1979 the Ryder Cup has been played for by teams representing the USA and Europe.

The Professional Golfers' Association was founded in 1901 to promote the interest in the game of golf and to protect and advance the mutual and trade interests of its members. The P.G.A. is the oldest such Association in the world and is responsible for promoting professional tournaments run under its auspices in the British Isles.

It is most advantageous for any beginner to the game to seek advice from any golf professional who is a member of the P.G.A. He will advise on correct equipment and give tuition on the basic fundamentals of the game which are described in this book; the book is essentially a guide to the game and is not meant to be a complete reference.

The official Rules of Golf are governed by The Royal and Ancient Golf Club of St. Andrews. This book is not meant to be a substitute for the official publication but should be read in conjunction with it. The Rules governing situations described in this book are shown in brackets at the end of each section. The Rules of Golf are published by Royal Insurance and are available free of charge from most golf clubs or by post from Royal Insurance (UK) Ltd, PO Box 144, New Hall Place, Liverpool L69 3EN.

If you have any doubt or query do not hesitate to ask your professional or Golf Club secretary for information; he will be only too pleased to give assistance. Irrespective of the degree of playing ability actually attained, golf is a pastime which can be enjoyed by young and old alike, and I have pleasure in recommending this book to all who wish to know the game of golf.

Colin Snape
Executive Director,
The Professional Golfers' Association

The Game of Golf

"The Game of Golf consists in playing a ball from the teeing ground into the hole by successive strokes in accordance with the Rules." (*Rule 1*)

A full-sized course consists of 18 holes, with usually four "short" holes, which measure up to 250 yards from tee to green and can be covered by one full stroke, and 14 longer holes, from 250 to 500 yards or more in length, and requiring two or three full strokes from tee to green. One round of the course is the usual length of a match, but in some competitions two or more rounds are played. One round occupies about three hours.

The space between tee and green at the long holes is occupied by mown turf called the "fairway" and on either side of the fairway are rough grass, trees, bushes, etc. There are also "hazards" of various kinds, mainly sand bunkers but occasionally streams, ditches, and ponds. The green is a closely mown surface for putting and the "hole" is sunk in the green and marked with a flag.

Etiquette

In addition to the rules, the game also has a code of etiquette, which should be observed by all golfers and studied with particular care by beginners. Adherence to these rules of behaviour helps to make the game more enjoyable for everyone. The rules of etiquette are quoted in full on page 35, but can be summarised as follows:

Do not move, talk, stand close to or directly behind the ball or the hole when a player is making a stroke.

Do not play until the match in front is out of range, but do not unnecessarily delay play.

If overtaken by a following match while searching for a ball, or because of your own slow play, signal to the overtaking players to pass, and then wait until they have gone out of range before continuing play.

Smooth over holes and footmarks made in bunker sand before leaving it, and see that all turf cut by the club-head is replaced and pressed down.

Avoid damage to greens by clubs, feet or flagstick, and repair marks made by the ball when landing. After placing flagstick walk off quickly when the result of the hole is determined, without re-trying putts, so that the way is clear for following players.

Wood club   grip   Iron club

shaft

neck   head
head   heel   socket
face   heel
sole   toe   face
toe   sole

The Club and the Ball

Two Rules prohibit the use of any club or ball which does not conform to clearly-defined specifications and fundamental principles of design. Clubs must have all the various parts fixed and not capable of adjustment. Concave faces are banned, also those having markings which do not satisfy the current requirements or are modified for the purpose of unduly influencing the movement of the ball.

The grip on the shaft may not have a channel or furrow or be moulded to the hands, and the shaft itself must be fixed to the heel of the club-head, except in the case of a putter. The shaft of a putter may be fixed at any point in the head but must be straight and must diverge from the vertical by at least ten degrees from a point not more than five inches above the sole.

An "iron" club is one with a head which is usually relatively narrow from face to back, and is usually made of steel. A "wood' club is one with a head relatively broad from face to back, and is usually made of wood, plastic, or a light metal. (*Rule 4*)

The weight of the ball shall be not greater than 1.62 ounces (45.9 grammes) and the size not less than 1.62 inches (41.2 mm) in diameter. The minimum diameter in the United States and some other countries is 1.68 inches (42.7 mm) and since 1968 this larger ball has been in use in

serrated and raised ribs

concave

more than the degree of defree of loft

depth greater than breadth

Some old-fashioned club heads now illegal

Centre-shafted

Modern examples of putters

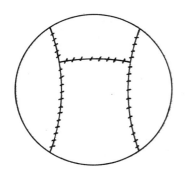

Old-fashioned ball stuffed with feathers

Guttie

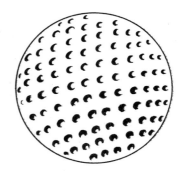

Rubber core

all tournaments run under the auspices of the PGA. There is also a velocity standard and only Balls on the approved lists of conforming Balls of the R. & A. and U.S.G.A. are legal. (*Rule 5*)

Discussions started in 1970 with the object of reaching a compromise between the British and American sizes and so achieving uniformity throughout the world.

Although golf in its earliest and unrecorded days was probably played with odd missiles such as pebbles or lumps of wood, the first ball known to history was the "featherie"—a leather bag stuffed tightly with feathers and then stitched. This was at best an ill-flying ball with a very short life, particularly in wet weather, but it re-mained in general use for more than two centuries until the advent of the "guttie" over a century ago. This was made from gutta-percha, softened and cast in a spherical mould, originally hand-hammered to make it fly straight. Later, moulds with embossed or recessed patterns came into use.

In the late 1890s the Haskell ball, made from strip rubber wound round a core, was produced in America, and first used in Britain in 1902. It soon ousted the guttie, and the rubber-core ball, as it is called, is now made to perfection by up-to-date machinery and with reasonable care will last for many rounds of golf without losing shape or resilience.

Preparing to hit the Ball

Stance

A player has "addressed the ball" when he has taken his stance and has also grounded his club (or, in a hazard, has taken his stance).

The stance, or position taken by the feet in preparing for the stroke, varies with the build of the player, his method of swinging, and the type of shot being attempted, but, generally speaking, the feet are straddled along a line which is parallel to the line of intended flight of the ball.

The width of the stance also varies with players and types of shot, but a good rule is to stand so that the distance between the feet is about equal to the width of the shoulders. As the shots to the green get shorter so the stance narrows. The whole idea should be to use the minimum width of stance consistent with good balance. Too wide a stance restricts the pivoting of the body. Too narrow a stance makes the body sway, which is disadvantageous.

There are three basic stances: Square, Open and Closed; and the one used depends upon the club chosen and the type of shot to be played.

THE SQUARE STANCE is used for most long shots with the woods and long irons.

THE OPEN STANCE mostly for bad lies, short shots, and approach play, etc.

THE CLOSED STANCE when it is necessary to put draw or hook on the ball.

Address

At the address position, the feet should be approximately as far apart as the width of the player's shoulders, with the weight evenly distributed between the feet: the toes should be pointed outwards very slightly and the knees flexed slightly inwards. The left arm, wrist and club should be virtually in a straight line, with the hands slightly ahead of the club-head. The body should not be too crouched or too upright in position, but just between the two.

Square stance, showing ball positions

DRIVER○
FAIRWAY WOODS ○
LONG IRONS ○
MIDDLE IRONS ○
SHORT IRONS ○

Open stance

TARGET

TARGET

Closed stance

9

Ball Placement

DRIVER: opposite the left heel.
FAIRWAY WOODS and
LONG IRONS: just inside the left heel.
MIDDLE IRONS: between the centre of the feet and the left heel, with the feet now getting closer together.
SHORT IRONS: midway between the feet which should now be about nine inches apart.

The next thing to consider is the distance from the ball. This depends again on the build of the golfer and the size of club used, but the guiding factor is comfort and relaxation. One should feel comfortably settled down for hitting the ball, neither over-reaching for it nor hunched up. For the driver a good tip is to rest the club-head behind the ball and stand so that the outstretched arm, holding the club, makes a straight line from shoulder to ball, while the body stands erect. Then bend forward to place the right hand on the shaft, and the position is correct. Another test is to take up a stance and then take away the right hand, dropping the club with the left until it touches the thigh above the left knee. This shows again that the distance is correct.

The Grip

Although there are several ways of gripping a club, some of them highly unorthodox, the grip most commonly used is the overlapping or "Vardon" grip, so called after its originator Harry Vardon, who won the Open Championship on a record six occasions between 1896 and 1914.

Commence by placing the left hand on the club: it must be a combination of finger and palm grip. The club must lie across the hands from the middle joint of the first finger, over the base of the middle finger and into the heel of the hand. When the hand is closed, the thumb should be a quarter of the way round the shaft to the right and the tip of the thumb in line with the knuckle of the first finger. The "V" formed between the thumb and first finger should point between the chin and the right shoulder.

The right hand is a finger grip. To help the two hands to work together the little finger of the right hand overlaps the first finger of the left hand.

The grip lies across the middle joint of the other three fingers and the palm of the right hand fits snugly over the left thumb. The "V" formed between the thumb and forefinger also points to a spot between the chin and the right shoulder. There should now be a firm and lively connection of the hands and the club-head.

The Vardon grip

Tommy Horton

Making the Stroke

A "stroke" is the forward movement of the club made with the intention of fairly striking at and moving the ball.

The mechanics of the golf swing consist in swinging the club backwards and upwards from the address position to a position above and behind the head from which a downward and forward blow can be aimed at the ball. The accompanying sketches should make clear the sequence of movements, but there are certain principles to bear in mind.

The club-head is taken back from the ball by a co-ordinated movement of various parts of the body, which pivots or turns on an axis formed by the spine. The hands lead, while the left heel may leave the ground, the left knee bends inwards and sideways and the shoulders and hips turn. The head remains still throughout the swing, the chin pointing towards the ball, and when the club-head is half-way up to the top of the swing position the wrists begin to bend or "cock". At the top of the swing the club shaft should be almost horizontal and the club head pointing at the target.

The start of the down-swing is a general "pull-down" of the left side, hands and arms leading, and then the rest of the down-swing is a progressive speeding up of the club-head, which is whipped into the ball in a flail-like manner. The whole movement, up and down, should be rhythmic and controlled.

A natural sequel to the down-swing is the "follow-through", in which the body turns in the direction of flight and the club-head is flung out in the same direction until at the finish of the stroke the trunk is square towards the hole, the hands high, and the club-shaft behind the back.

The golf swing is more or less the same for all maximum-length shots, no matter what club is used, but in the case of short pitches or run-up shots when near to the green the back-swing must be restricted according to the length of the shot. This can only be judged by practice and experience.

The Rules of the Game

loft   approximate distances

Number of clubs allowed

The player cannot start a round with more than 14 clubs. He may replace any club which becomes unfit for play in the normal course of play but such replacement may not be made by borrowing from any other person playing on the course. (Penalty: Match Play: Loss of hole for each hole at which violation occurred with a maximum of two holes. Stroke Play: Two strokes for each hole at which violation occurred with a maximum of four strokes.)

A complete "matched set" of 14 clubs can be obtained, consisting usually of either four woods, nine irons and a putter or three woods, ten irons and a putter, depending on the individual preference of the player.

The length of a golf club varies from roughly 42 inches for a driver to 35 inches for a short iron or putter, diminishing at half-inch intervals. As the club diminishes in length, so the club face increases in weight and angle of loft, e.g. the driver, at 42 inches has an angle of loft on its face of 11 degrees, the five iron at 38 inches has an angle of loft on its face of 30 degrees, and the wedge at 36 inches has an angle of 52 degrees. Women's clubs are lighter and slightly shorter than those used by men, and matched sets are "fitted" to the players, some requiring lighter or shorter clubs than the standard sizes, or shafts with varying degrees of "whip". (*Rule 4.4*)

Agreement to waive the rules is prohibited

Players must not agree among themselves to waive a Rule or a Local Rule or any penalty incurred. (*Rule 1–3*)

General penalty

Except when otherwise provided for, the penalty for a breach of a rule shall be the loss of a hole in match play or two strokes in stroke play.

Note: This is the usual penalty but certain minor infringements incur a penalty of one stroke. Generally speaking, disqualification occurs only in the case of deliberate infringement. (*Rules 2–6 and 3–5*)

Types of Play

Match play

In match play a hole is won by the side which holes its ball in the fewest strokes (after deducting any handicap allowance). The hole is halved if each side holes out in the same number of strokes. A match consists of a stipulated round or rounds, and is won by the side which is leading by a number of holes greater than the number remaining to be played.

Note: Thus, if a side is four up after playing 15 holes, they have won the match by four up and three to play (usually written as 4 & 3). If, after finishing the eighteenth hole, each side has won an equal number, the match is halved. If a decision is essential, as in a knock-out tournament or championship, it is usual for the players to begin the round again, the first to win a hole taking the match. Thus a game can be won at the 19th, the 20th and so on. In playing additional holes, handicap strokes are given and taken at the same holes as in the first round. (*Rule 2*)

Stroke play

The competitor who holes the stipulated round or rounds in the fewest strokes is the winner.

Note: In stroke competitions under handicap the full handicap allowed the player is deducted from his total, and the net score counts. (*Rule 3*)

Practice during play

During the play of a hole a player must not play any practice stroke. Between the play of two holes a player cannot play a practice stroke from any hazard, or on to a putting green other than that of the hole last played. On any day of a stroke competition or play-off, the competitor shall not practise on the competition course before a round or play-off. When a competition extends over consecutive days or on different courses, practice on any competition course still to be played between rounds is prohibited.

It is important to note that a practice swing is not a practice stroke, as a stroke is a forward movement of the club with the intention of striking a ball. (*Rule 7*)

Advice and assistance during play

A player may only give advice to, or ask advice from, his partner or either of their caddies. In making a stroke a player must not seek or accept physical assistance or protection from the weather. A player may have the line of play indicated by anyone (except on the putting green, where only the player's partner or caddie may do so), but no one shall place a mark or stand to indicate the line of play while the stroke is being played.

Note: "Assistance" or "protection" includes bending back an obstructing bush or shielding a player from wind or rain. (*Rules 8 and 14–2*)

Information as to strokes taken

A player who has incurred a penalty must tell his opponent or marker as soon as possible. The number of strokes a player has taken shall include any penalty strokes incurred. A player in match play is entitled at any time during the play of a hole to ask the number of strokes his opponent has taken. If the opponent gives wrong information and fails to correct the mistake before the player has played his next stroke, the opponent shall lose the hole. (*Rule 9*)

Disputes, decisions and doubts as to rights

In match play where there is a dispute about the Rules or the number of strokes taken, a claim must be made before the players strike off from the next teeing ground or (in the case of the last hole of the match) before they leave the putting green. Any later claim based on newly discovered facts cannot be considered unless the player making the claim had been given the wrong information by an opponent. In stroke play no penalty shall be imposed after the results are posted or prizes presented, unless the player knowingly returns a score for a hole lower than actually achieved. If a referee has been appointed by the Committee, his decision shall be final. In the absence of a referee, the decision of the Committee shall be final. If the Committee cannot come to a decision, it shall refer to the Rules of Golf Committee of the Royal and Ancient Golf Club of St. Andrews and its decision shall be final.

If any point in dispute be not covered by the Rules or Local Rules, the decision shall be made in accordance with fair play and logic which is referred to in golf as "equity".

In stroke play a competitor who is unsure of his rights or the correct procedure may play out the hole with the original ball and, at the same time, complete the play of the hole with a second ball stating which ball he wishes to score with if that procedure is allowable under the rules. The point is then referred to the committee for adjudication. If a player fails to state which ball he wants to count, the ball with higher score (if allowable under the rules) will count. This does not apply to Match Play. (*Rules 2–5, 3–3 and 34*)

Order of play on the tee – "The Honour"

A match begins by each side playing a ball from the first teeing ground in order of the draw or by lot. The side which wins a hole takes "the honour", i.e. plays first, at the next teeing ground. In match play an opponent may recall a ball played out of turn, but in stroke play the stroke must stand. In neither case is there any penalty. (*Rule 10*)

The teeing ground

The teeing ground is the starting place for the hole to be played. It is a rectangular area two club-lengths in depth, the front and the sides of which are defined by the outside limits of two markers. A ball is outside the teeing ground when all of it lies outside the area defined above.

Note: The teeing ground is not necessarily the whole of the flat space prepared for teeing, but only that part in use for the day. The position of the markers is varied from day to day to avoid undue wear and tear of any one particular area. (*Rule 11*)

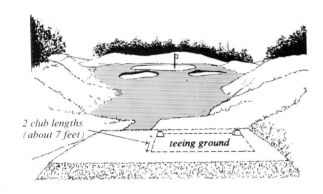

The hole

The "hole" must be $4\frac{1}{4}$ inches (108 mm) in diameter and at least 4 inches (100 mm) deep. If a lining is used it shall be sunk at least 1 inch (25 mm) below the putting green surface unless the nature of the soil makes it impractical to do so. Its outer diameter shall not exceed $4\frac{1}{4}$ inches (108 mm). (*See Definitions*)

Playing outside the teeing ground

If a player in a match, when starting a hole, plays a ball from outside the teeing ground there is no penalty, but his opponent may require him to play the stroke again from within the teeing ground. In stroke play, however, he shall be penalised two strokes and must play the stroke again from the correct place. Strokes played by a competitor from outside the teeing ground do not count in his score. If a competitor fails to rectify his mistake before making a stroke off the next teeing ground or, in the case of the last hole of the round, before leaving the putting green, he shall be disqualified.

A player may take his stance outside the teeing ground to play a ball within it. (*Rule 11*)

Ball falling off tee

If a ball, when not in play (that is, when a stroke has not yet been made at it) falls off the tee, or is knocked off by the player, in addressing it, it may be re-teed without penalty. (*Rule 11–2*)

Order of play in threesome and foursome

In a foursome (two players playing one ball against a similar pair) the partners shall strike off alternately from the teeing grounds (*A* drives at the first hole and *B* at the second, etc.) and thereafter the partners shall strike alternately during the play of each hole. In match play if a player plays when his partner should have played, his side loses the hole. **The penalty in stroke play is two strokes, or disqualification if the stroke is not rectified by replaying the stroke in the correct order. (*Rule 29*)**

Ball played as it lies

The ball shall be played as it lies at all times except where the Rules or Local Rules provide otherwise. (*Rule 13–1*)

Ball falling of tee – no penalty

Improving lie or stance and influencing ball prohibited

Irregularities of surface which could affect a player's lie may not be removed or pressed down by the player, his partner, or either of their caddies except (*a*) as may occur in fairly taking his stance, (*b*) in making the stroke or the backward movement of his club for the stroke, (*c*) when teeing a ball or (*d*) repairing damage to the putting green.

If the ball lies in long grass, rushes, bushes, whins, heather or the like, only so much shall be touched as will enable the player to find and identify his ball: nothing shall be done which can in any way improve its lie.

A player may not improve, or allow to be improved, his line of play, the position or lie of his ball, or the area of his intended swing, by bending, moving or breaking anything fixed or growing (except in taking a fair stance to address the ball, and in making the stroke). (*Rules 13–2 and 12–1*)

Loose impediments

A loose impediment may be removed without penalty except when both the impediment and the ball lie in or touch a hazard. When a ball is moving a loose impediment on his line of play shall not be removed. (*Rule 23*)

The term "loose impediments" includes natural objects not fixed or growing and not sticking to the ball, e.g. stones not solidly embedded, leaves, twigs, branches and the like, dung, worms and insects and casts or heaps made by them.

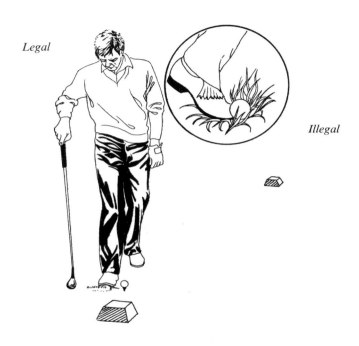

Legal

Illegal

Improving lie or stance prohibited except on tee

19

Snow and ice are either casual water or loose impediments, at the option of the player. Dew, however, is not a loose impediment.

Sand and loose soil are loose impediments on the putting green, but not elsewhere on the course. (*See Definitions*)

Striking at the ball
The ball shall be firmly struck at with the head of the club, and must not be pushed, scraped or spooned.

If a player, when making a stroke, strikes the ball twice he shall count the stroke and add a penalty stroke—making two strokes in all. (*Rule 14*)

Illegal

Scoop – illegal

Ball farther from the hole played first

When the balls are in play the ball farthest from the hole shall be played first. In match play, if a player plays when his opponent should have done so, the opponent may immediately require the player to replay the stroke. In stroke-play no penalty is incurred and the ball shall be played as it lies. (*Rule 10*)

Playing a wrong ball or playing from a wrong place

A player must hole out with the ball driven from the teeing ground unless he has substituted his ball with another under the Rules or Local Rules.

Note: Generally there is a penalty of two strokes in stroke play or loss of hole in match play for playing the wrong ball, but if a player in a stroke competition holes out with the wrong ball he is disqualified, unless he rectifies his mistake by finding and holing out with his own ball from the place where the mistake occurred, provided he has not played a stroke from the next teeing ground. In match play if each side plays the other side's ball and it cannot be settled which side first committed the error, the hole shall be played out with the balls thus exchanged. (*Rule 15*)

Lifting, dropping, placing, identifying or cleaning ball

Through the green or in a hazard, when a ball is lifted under a Rule or Local Rule or when another ball is to be played, it shall be lifted and dropped as near as possible to the spot where the ball lay, except when a rule permits it to be dropped elsewhere or placed. In a hazard, a lifted ball must be dropped and come to rest in the hazard; if it rolls out of the hazard it must be re-dropped without penalty. (If on a putting green the ball shall be placed.)

A ball may only be dropped by the player himself. He shall stand erect, hold the ball at shoulder height with outstretched arm and at arm's length and drop it. If a ball is dropped in any other way the player shall incur a penalty stroke. If the ball touches the player before it strikes the ground, the player shall re-drop without penalty. If the ball touches his partner or either of their caddies or equipment before or after it strikes the ground the ball shall be re-dropped without penalty.

A ball to be lifted under the rules may be lifted by the player or his partner, or by another person authorised by the player. It may be lifted for the purpose of identification but must then be replaced on the same spot. A ball may be cleaned when lifted from an unplayable lie, for relief from an obstruction, from casual water, or ground under repair, from a water hazard, on a wrong green, or on the putting green. Otherwise during the play of the hole a player may not clean a ball except to the extent necessary for identification or if permitted by Local Rules. (*Rules 12–2, 20 and 21*)

Ball interfering with play

Anywhere on the course a player may have any other ball lifted if he considers that it might interfere with his play. A ball so lifted shall be replaced after the player has played his stroke. If a ball is accidentally moved when complying with this rule, no penalty shall be incurred, but the ball so moved shall be replaced. (*Rule 22*)

A moving ball

A player shall not play while his ball is moving, with the exception of certain cases, e.g. when the ball is moving in water, provided he hits the ball without delay, thus not allowing wind or current to better his position. (*Rule 14–5*)

Penalty—player's ball deflected by caddie (see page 23)

Lifting a ball

Ball in motion stopped or deflected

If a ball in motion is accidentally stopped or deflected by any outside agency, it is a "rub of the green" and the ball shall be played as it lies, without penalty.

If it lodges in anything moving, a ball shall be dropped through the green or in a hazard, or placed on the putting green, as near as possible to the spot where the moving object was when the ball lodged in it, without penalty.

If the player's ball in motion is stopped or deflected by him, his partner or either of their caddies, or their clubs or other equipment, the player or his side shall be penalised two strokes in stroke play or lose the hole in match play. (*Rule 19*)

Ball at rest moved

If a ball at rest is moved or the lie altered by a fellow-competitor or the caddie or any outside agency, the player shall replace the ball, without penalty to himself. If it is impossible to determine the exact spot, the ball shall be dropped (or placed on the putting green) as near as possible to the place from which it was moved, and not nearer the hole.

Except while searching for the ball, if it is moved by the opponent in match play the opponent shall incur a penalty stroke, and the ball shall be replaced. If it is moved by the player whether while searching or not, he shall incur a

penalty stroke, and the ball shall be replaced. In stroke play if the ball is moved by a fellow competitor, there is no penalty but the ball must be restored to its original position, but if the ball is moved by the player he shall incur a penalty stroke. (*Rule 18*)

Outside agency – no penalty, ball replaced

Ball accidentally moved – if by player, partner, caddie or equipment 1 stroke penalty, if by anyone else no penalty

23

Ball unplayable

by him, adding a penalty stroke to his score for the hole. A ball may be declared unplayable at any place on the course except in a water hazard, and the player is the sole judge as to whether his ball is unplayable. If a player decides his ball is unplayable he shall either (*a*) play his next stroke as provided for a ball lost or out of bounds, i.e. the "stroke and distance" penalty, or (*b*) drop a ball, under a penalty of one stroke, either within two club-lengths of the point where the ball lay, but not nearer the hole; or behind the point where the ball lay, keeping that point between himself and the hole, with no limit to how far behind that point the ball may be dropped. If the ball lay in a bunker, a ball must be dropped in the bunker, if relief is taken under Clause (b). (*Rules 27 and 28*)

Ball unfit for play

If a ball in play is so badly damaged that it becomes unfit for further play it may be changed by the player after agreeing with his opponent or marker that it is so damaged. Mud on a ball does not make it unfit for play. If a ball breaks into pieces as a result of a stroke, it shall be replaced with another ball without penalty. (*Rule 5–3*)

Ball lost, out of bounds or unplayable

If a ball is lost outside a water hazard or is out of bounds, the player shall play his next stroke as nearly as possible at the spot from which the original ball was played or moved

Out of bounds

24

Eamonn Darcy watches his fellow-competitor Steve Elkington measuring the distance to drop his ball from an unplayable lie.

Provisional ball (*See Definitions*)

If a ball may be lost outside a water hazard or may be out of bounds, to save time the player may at once play another ball provisionally as nearly as possible from the spot at which the original ball was played. Before playing a provisional ball the player must announce his intention to his opponent or marker, and such a ball may be played only before the player or his partner goes forward to search for the original ball. The player may play a provisional ball until he reaches the place where the original ball is likely to be. If he plays any strokes with the provisional ball from the point beyond that place, the original ball is deemed to be lost, even if it is later found. If the original ball be lost outside a water hazard or be out of bounds he shall continue play with the provisional ball under penalty of stroke and distance. If the original ball be unplayable in bounds, or lie or be lost in a water hazard, the provisional ball shall be abandoned. (*Rule 27–2*)

Obstructions (*See Definitions*)

Any movable obstruction may be removed before a shot is played. If the obstruction is immovable, or the ball lies on or touches the movable obstruction, the ball may be lifted and dropped not more than one club-length away from the point where relief is obtained, such point is determined as the nearest point to where the ball lay, without penalty, and must come to rest not nearer the hole. (*Rule 24*)

Casual water

If a player's ball lies in or touches casual water, ground under repair or a hole, cast or runway made by a burrowing animal, a reptile or a bird, or if any of these conditions interfere with the player's stance or the area of his intended swing ... he may drop a ball without penalty on ground which avoids these conditions, within one club-length of the point where the player gets relief, such point shall be determined as the nearest point to where the ball lay. He may also drop a ball similarly in a hazard **without penalty; if a ball is dropped clear of the hazard there is a penalty stroke.**

Ball on drain cover (immovable obstruction)

Immovable obstruction. Ball may be dropped within one club length (c) of the nearest point of relief (b)

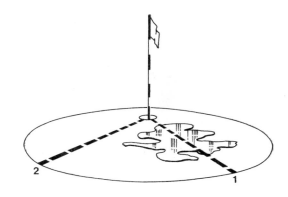

Casual water – ball may be moved from 1 to 2

If a ball lies on the putting green and in casual water, or if casual water intervenes between it and the hole, the ball may be lifted and placed, without penalty, on the nearest spot (not nearer the hole) which will give a clear line to the hole. (*Rule 25*)

Hazards and water hazards (*See Definitions*)

When the ball lies in or touches a hazard or water hazard nothing shall be done which can in any way improve its lie. Before making a stroke, the player shall not touch the ground or water with his club, nor touch or move any loose impediment in the hazard.

If the ball lies or is lost in a water hazard, the player can play the ball as it lies, or, under a penalty of one stroke, drop a ball: (*a*) behind the water hazard, without limit as to distance, keeping the spot at which the ball last crossed the margin of the hazard between himself and the hole, or (*b*) as near as possible to the spot from which the original ball was played.

A player may drop a ball outside a lateral water hazard within two club-lengths of the margin of either side, opposite the point where the ball last crossed the hazard margin. The ball must come to rest not nearer the hole than this point.

Note: Hazards are of various kinds, but bunkers form by far the greatest number of such hazards on most golf course. Bunkers are depressions in the ground filled with sand, and usually built up on the side nearest the hole, so

Water hazard

Touching ground with club before stroke prohibited

27

that the player must loft the ball out, thus losing considerable distance in relation to an opponent lying on the fairway. Most bunkers however, are around the greens, and considerable skill is required to get the ball out and near enough to the hole to have a chance of **getting down in one putt.** (*Rule 13–4 and 26*)

Scraping sand to see top of ball

The flagstick

The flagstick

Before or during the stroke, the player may have the flagstick removed or held up to indicate the position of the hole, at any time. This may be done only on the authority of the player before he plays his stroke. If the flagstick is attended or removed by an opponent, a fellow-competitor, or the caddie of either, with the knowledge of the player, and no objection is made, the player shall be deemed to have authorised it.

If a player's ball strikes the flagstick when it is attended or has been removed, or if it strikes the person standing at the flagstick or equipment carried by him, or if it strikes an unattended flagstick when played from the putting green, the player shall incur a penalty of loss of hole in match play or two strokes in stroke play.

If the ball is played from off the green and comes to rest against the flagstick when it is in the hole, the player shall be entitled to have the flagstick removed, and if the ball falls into the hole the player shall be deemed to have holed out at his last stroke. (*Rule 17*)

Flagstick being held to indicate position of hole

The putting green

The line of the putt must not be touched except as provided in the Rules, but the player may place the club in front of the ball when addressing it, without pressing anything down. The player may move any loose impediment on the putting green by picking it up or brushing it aside with his hand or a club, without pressing anything down. If the ball is moved, it shall be replaced, without penalty.

The player may repair damage to the putting green caused by the impact of a ball and old hole plugs. The ball may be marked and lifted to permit repair and shall be replaced on the spot from which it was lifted.

A ball lying on the putting green may be marked and lifted without penalty, cleaned if desired, and replaced on the spot from which it was lifted.

When the ball nearer the hole lies on the putting green, if the player considers it might interfere with his play, he may require the opponent to mark and lift the ball, which must be replaced after the player has played his stroke.

Anyone on the player's side may, before a stroke is made, point out a line for putting, but the following are prohibited:

Placing a mark on the green; touching line of putt in front of, to the side of, or behind the hole; testing surface of green or rolling a ball on it or roughening or scraping the surface; playing before the other ball is at rest; standing so as to influence position or movement of the ball; lifting other ball while player's ball is in motion.

A ball lying on a putting green other than that of the hole being played must be lifted and dropped off the putting green, not nearer the hole, without penalty, as near as possible to where the ball lay.

The player shall not make a stroke on the putting green from a stance astride, or with either foot touching the line of the putt or an extension of the line behind the ball.

Loose impediments may be removed

Pitch marks may be repaired

Match Play: Putting out of turn: the opponent may require the stroke to be replayed, in match play.

A ball moved by another ball must be replaced.

In match play a player after holing out may remove his opponent's ball, provided it is at rest, claiming the hole or conceding the half as the case may be. If the opponent's ball is not removed and it falls into the hole, the opponent is deemed to have holed out at his last stroke.

Stroke Play: In stroke play if the ball nearer the hole is in the way or affecting the playing of the other ball in any way, it may be played first or marked and lifted while the other ball is played, but only at the request of the player about to putt.

In stroke play the ball may be lifted or putted first if the owner considers it might be of assistance to a fellow competitor.

When both balls lie on the putting green, if the competitor's ball strikes the other he shall incur a penalty of two strokes and play the ball as it lies. The other ball shall at once be replaced. (*Rules 16 and 19*)

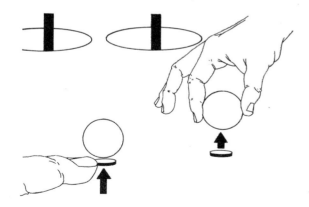

Lifting the ball is allowed

Prohibited – touching line of putt in front of, to side of, or behind the hole

Roger Chapman

Putting

Putting is the most precise part of the game and arguably the most important, for strokes can be saved by good putting and wasted by bad putting. The normal average allowance is two putts per green, but a golfer who is putting well usually beats this average.

When the ball lies a fair distance from the hole the stroke is called an "approach putt", and demands accurate judgement of strength and line. If the green at that part is level, it may be a "straight putt", but more often the stroke requires a "borrow" (the ball is then aimed at a point to right or left to allow for the slope).

Then the player must estimate the strength of the putt. If the green slopes down towards the hole, less power will be required than if the putt is uphill. Again, the green might be "slow" after rain or because the grass has grown, or "fast" because of hot sunshine or strong wind. This is one area of the game where the Vardon grip is not used and is replaced by a grip with the thumb directly down the handle.

Having summed up the situation to his own satisfaction, the player makes a trial swing to make sure he has the desired stroke well in mind, and then gets his putter blade at right-angles to the intended line and immediately behind the ball. He takes a short or long back-swing, according to the type of stroke, and delivers a firm smooth stroke, keeping the putter blade as far as possible on the line intended.

Putting

Keeping the Score

Cards like the specimen shown on page 34 are used for marking a competitor's score in a Medal, Stableford or Match Play Against Par (Bogey) competition. In Medal play the competitor's full handicap is deducted from his total score. In Stableford competitions seven-eighths of the handicap is taken and in Match Play Against Par (Bogey) competitions three-quarters of the handicap is taken. In matches the player with the higher handicap receives three-quarters of the difference between his handicap and that of his opponent.

Column 1   gives No. of hole.

Column 2   gives length of hole, measured from competition tees.

Column 3   gives the par of the hole.

Column 4   indicates where handicap strokes are taken in Match Play Against Par (Bogey) or Stableford competitions. For example, a player having 12 strokes takes one at the 5th (numbered 12) and one each at all other holes having figures less than 12. A player having only three strokes takes them at the 2nd, 9th and 14th holes.

Column 5 is for the player's score in strokes. This is always given as the gross score, the number of strokes actually played and inserted by marker. Handicap calculations are made afterwards.

Column 6 shows the result of each hole compared with par. If the player's net score for the hole (after deducting any handicap stroke) is less than the par score he marks " + " indicating a win. If the score is the same the Committee marks "0", indicating a halved hole. If the score is higher the Committe marks " — " indicating a loss.

The card shown on previous page is marked out for a player having gone round in 71 net, and finishing one over par in stroke play competition, or finishing all square in a Match Play Against Par (Bogey) competition. The stars indicate those items which are the Committee's responsibility. Both the player and marker *must* sign the card before it is handed in.

LOCKHEATH GOLF CLUB

STANDARD SCRATCH SCORE 70   Date 1/1/85 *

Handicap 16 *

Player J. SNOOKS * Competition Bogey   Strokes Received 12 *

Hole	Yards	Par	Stroke Index	Players Score	Won/Lost/Halved	Hole	Yards	Par	Stroke Index	Players Score	Won/Lost/Halved
1	460	4	14	7	— *	10	350	4	- 11	6	— *
2	390	4	- 3	4	+ *	11	350	4	- 6	4	+ *
3	430	4	16	6	— *	12	165	3	15	3	0 *
4	195	3	- 7	3	+ *	13	510	5	-10	6	0 *
5	335	4	-12	5	0 *	14	360	4	- 2	5	0 *
6	480	5	- 5	6	0 *	15	345	4	- 8	4	+ *
7	350	4	- 9	4	+ *	16	140	3	17	4	— *
8	115	3	18	6	— *	17	400	4	- 4	5	0 *
9	360	4	- 1	5	0 *	18	295	4	13	4	0 *
OUT	3115	35		46	*	IN	2915	35		41	*

Markers Signature M. Smith

Competitors Signature J. Snooks

Bogey
Holes Won 5
Holes Lost 5   *
Holes Halved 8
Result ALL SQUARE

OUT	3115	35		46 *
	6030	70		87 *
HANDICAP......				16 *
NET SCORE.....				71 *

Readers are strongly advised to read the Rules of Golf in full, but for their information Sections I and II concerning Etiquette and Definitions, are reproduced here.

Etiquette

Courtesy On The Course

Consideration for other players

In the interest of all, players should play without delay.

No player should play until the players in front are out of range.

Players searching for a ball should signal the players behind them to pass as soon as it becomes apparent that the ball will not easily be found; they should not search for five minutes before doing so. They should not continue play until the players following them have passed and are out of range.

When play of a hole has been completed, players should immediately leave the putting green.

Behaviour during play

No one should move, talk or stand close to or directly behind the ball or the hole when a player is addressing the ball or making a stroke.

The player who has the honour should be allowed to play before his opponent or fellow-competitor tees his ball.

Priority On The Course

In the absence of special rules, two-ball matches should have precedence of and be entitled to pass any three- or four-ball matches.

A single player has no standing and should give way to a match of any kind.

Any match playing a whole round is entitled to pass a match playing a shorter round.

If a match fails to keep its place on the course and loses more than one clear hole on the players in front, it should allow the match following to pass.

Care Of The Course

Holes in bunkers

Before leaving a bunker, a player should carefully fill up and smooth over all holes and footprints made by him.

Restore divots, repair ball-marks and spike-marks

Through the green, a player should ensure that any turf cut or displaced by him is replaced at once and pressed down, and that any damage to the putting green made by the ball or the player is carefully repaired. Damage to the putting green by golf-shoe spikes should be repaired on completion of the hole.

Damage to greens—flagsticks, bags, etc.

Players should ensure that, when putting down bags, or the flagstick, no damage is done to the putting green, and that neither they nor their caddies damage the hole by standing close to it, in handling the flagstick or in removing the ball from the hole. The flagstick should be properly replaced in the hole before the players leave the putting green. Players should not damage putting greens by leaning on their putters, particularly when removing the ball from the hole.

Golf carts
Local notices regulating the movement of golf carts should be strictly observed.

Damage through practice swings
In taking practice swings players should avoid causing damage to the course, particularly to tees, by removing divots.

Definitions

Addressing the ball
A player has "addressed the ball" when he has taken his stance and has also grounded his club, except that in a hazard a player has addressed the ball when he has taken his stance.

Advice
"Advice" is any counsel or suggestion which could influence a player in determining his play, the choice of a club, or the method of making a stroke.

Information on the Rules or Local Rules, or on matters of public information such as the position of hazards or the flagstick on the putting green, is not advice.

Ball deemed to move
A ball is deemed to have "moved" if it leaves its position and comes to rest in any other place.

Ball in play, provisional ball, wrong ball
a. A ball is "in play" as soon as the player has made a stroke on the teeing ground. It remains as his ball in play until holed out, except when it is out of bounds, lost or lifted, or another ball has been substituted under applicable Rule or Local Rule: a ball so substituted becomes the ball in play.

b. A "provisional ball" is a ball played under Rule 27–2 for a ball which may be lost outside a water hazard or may be out of bounds. It ceases to be a provisional ball when the Rule provides either that the player continues play with it as the ball in play or that it be abandoned.

c. A "wrong ball" is any ball other than the ball in play or a provisional ball or, in stroke play, a second ball in accordance with Rule 3–3 or 20–7b.

Ball lost
A ball is "lost" if:

a. It is not found, or is not identified as his by the player, within five minutes after the player's side or his or their caddies have begun to search for it; or

b. The player has put another ball into play under the Rules, even though he may not have searched for the original ball; or

c. The player has played any stroke with a provisional ball from a point nearer the hole than the place where the original ball is likely to be, whereupon the provisional ball becomes the ball in play.

Time spent in playing a wrong ball is not counted in the five-minute period allowed for search.

Caddie

a. A "caddie" is one who carries or handles a player's clubs during play and otherwise assists him in accordance with the Rules.

When one caddie is employed by more than one player, he is always deemed to be the caddie of the player whose ball is involved, and equipment carried by him is deemed to be that player's equipment, except when the caddie acts upon specific directions from another player, in which case he is considered to be that other player's caddie.

Casual water

"Casual water" is any temporary accumulation of water which is visible before or after the player takes his stance and which is not in a water hazard. Snow and ice are either casual water or loose impediments, at the option of the player. Dew is not casual water.

Committee

The "Committee" is the committee in charge of the competition, or, if the matter does not arise in a competition, the committee in charge of the course.

Competitor

A "competitor" is a player in a stroke competition. A "fellow-competitor" is any person with whom the competitor plays. Neither is partner of the other. In stroke play foursome and four-ball competitions, where the context so admits, the word "competitor" or "fellow-competitor" shall be held to include his partner.

Course

The "course" is the whole area within which play is permitted. (*Rule 33–2*)

Equipment

"Equipment" is anything used, worn or carried by or for the player except any ball he has played and any small object, such as a coin or a tee, when used to mark the position of a ball or the extent of an area in which a ball is to be dropped. Equipment includes a golf cart, whether or not motorised. If such a cart is shared by more than one player, its status under the Rules is the same as that of a caddie employed by more than one player. See "Caddie".

Flagstick

The "flagstick" is a movable straight indicator provided

by the Committee, with or without bunting or other material attached, centred in the hole to show its position. It shall be circular in cross-section.

Forecaddie
A "forecaddie" is one who is employed by the Committee to indicate to players the position of balls on the course, and is an "outside agency".

Ground under repair
"Ground under repair" is any portion of the course so marked by order of the committee concerned or so declared by its authorised representative. It includes material piled for removal and a hole made by a greenkeeper, even if not so marked. Stakes and lines defining ground under repair are in such ground.

Note 1: Grass cuttings and other material left on the course which have been abandoned and are not intended to be removed are not ground under repair unless so marked.

Note 2: The Committee may make a Local Rule prohibiting play from ground under repair.

Hazards
A "hazard" is any bunker or water hazard.

Hole
The "hole" shall be $4\frac{1}{4}$ inches (108 mm) in diameter and at least 4 inches (100 mm) deep. If a lining is used, it shall be sunk at least 1 inch (25 mm) below the putting green surface unless the nature of the soil makes it impracticable to do so; its outer diameter shall not exceed $4\frac{1}{4}$ inches (108 mm).

Holed
A ball is "holed" when it lies within the circumference of the hole and all of it is below the level of the lip of the hole.

Honour
The side which is entitled to play first from the teeing grounds is said to have the "honour".

Lateral water hazard
A "lateral water hazard" is a water hazard or that part of a water hazard so situated that it is not possible, or is deemed by the Committee to be impracticable, to drop a ball behind the water hazard and keep the spot at which the ball last crossed the hazard margin between the player and the hole. That part of the water hazard to be played as a lateral water hazard should be distinctively marked.

Note: Lateral water hazards should be defined by red stakes or lines.

Loose impediments
The term "loose impediments" denotes natural objects not fixed or growing and not adhering to the ball, and includes stones not solidly embedded, leaves, twigs, branches, and the like, dung, worms and insects and casts

or heaps made by them. Snow and ice are either casual water or loose impediments, at the option of the player.

Sand and loose soil are loose impediments on the putting green, but not elsewhere on the course.

Lost ball – *See* **Ball lost**

Marker

A "marker" is a scorer in stroke play who is appointed by the Committee to record a competitor's score. He may be a fellow-competitor. He is not a referee. A marker should not lift a ball or mark its position unless authorised to do so by the competitor and, unless he is a fellow-competitor, should not attend the flagstick or stand at the hole or mark its position.

Matches – *See* **Sides and Matches**

Observer

An "observer" is appointed by the Committee to assist a referee to decide questions of fact and to report to him any breach of a Rule or Local Rule. An observer should not attend the flagstick, stand at or mark the position of the hole, or lift the ball or mark its position.

Obstructions

An "obstruction" is anything artificial, whether erected, placed or left on the course, including artificial surfaces of roads and paths, but excepting:

a. Objects defining out of bounds, such as walls, fences, stakes and railings;
b. Any part of an immovable artificial object which is out of bounds;
c. Any construction declared by the Committee to be an integral part of the course.

Out of bounds

"Out of Bounds" is ground on which play is prohibited.

When out of bounds is defined by reference to stakes or a fence, the out of bounds line is determined by the nearest inside points of the stakes or fence posts at ground level excluding angled supports. When out of bounds is fixed by a line on the grounds the line itself is out of bounds.

A ball is out of bounds when all of it lies out of bounds.

The out of bounds line is deemed to extend vertically upwards and downwards.

The player may stand out of bounds to play a ball lying within bounds.

Outside agency

An "outside agency" is any agency not part of the match or, in stroke play, not part of a competitor's side, and includes a referee, a marker, an observer, or a forecaddie.

Neither wind nor water is an outside agency.

Partner

A "partner" is a player associated with another player on the same side. In a threesome, foursome or a four-ball where the context so admits, the word "player" shall be held to include his partner.

Penalty stroke

A "penalty stroke" is one added to the score of a side under certain Rules. In a threesome or foursome, penalty strokes do not affect the order of play.

Provisional ball

A "provisional ball" is a ball played under Rule 27–2 for a ball which may be lost outside a water hazard or may be out of bounds. It ceases to be a provisional ball when the Rule provides either that the player continue play with it as the ball in play or that it be abandoned.

Putting green

The "putting green" is all ground of the hole being played which is specially prepared for putting or otherwise defined as such by the Committee.

A ball is deemed to be on the putting green when any part of it touches the putting green.

Referee

A "referee" is one who is appointed by the Committee to accompany the players to decide questions of fact and apply the Rules of Golf. He shall act on any breach of Rule or Local Rule which he may observe or which may be reported to him.

A referee should not attend the flagstick, stand at or mark the position of the hole or lift the ball or mark its position.

Rub of the green

A "rub of the green" occurs when a ball in motion is stopped or deflected by any outside agency. (*Rule 19–1*)

Sides and matches

Side	A player or two or more players who are partners.
Single	A match in which one plays against another.
Threesome	A match in which one plays against two, and each side plays one ball.
Foursome	A match in which two play against two, and each side plays one ball.
Three-ball	A match in which three play against one another, each playing his own ball.
Best-ball	A match in which one plays against the better ball of two or the best ball of three players.
Four-ball	A match in which two play their better ball against the better ball of two other players.

Note: In a best-ball or four-ball match, if a partner is absent for reasons satisfactory to the Committee, the remaining member(s) of his side may represent the side.

Stance

Taking the "stance" consists in a player placing his feet in position for and preparatory to making a stroke.